Praise for
Savvy Networking for Nurses

"*Savvy Networking for Nurses* is a concise, helpful, and encouraging resource for today's nursing professional. Even as a seasoned nurse entrepreneur, I found exceptional insights and advice in Nurse Keith's first book focused on nurses' careers."

—**Beth Boynton,** MS, RN, Author of *Confident Voices: The Nurse's Guide to Improving Communication and Creating Positive Workplaces,* BethBoynton.com

"Here's why you made the right choice by taking the first step in reading this book, *Savvy Networking For Nurses*: networking is a teachable skill; it really is. You've also taken a great step forward by going on this journey with Keith Carlson, because I speak from experience when I say that if there's a teachable moment in your career, Keith is going to help guide you there. He truly has a gift to distill the information you need in order to find success."

—**Kevin Ross,** RN, BSN, Entrepreneur, Investor, Speaker, and Nurse CEO and Founder of Spire Health Partners, Inc., InnovativeNurse.com

"Keith Carlson is a master networker and career coach. In his book, *Savvy Networking for Nurses*, he provides the reader with simple strategies, tips, and tools to help nurses achieve career success. Keith uses simple yet powerful strategies to help nurses build global and hometown relationships. Knowing that the #1 desired human emotion is to feel connected with other humans, Keith provides the quintessential roadmap for success."

—**Dr. Renee Thompson**, DNP, RN, CMSRN, CEO and President of RTConnections, RTConnections.com

"Networking is a must for any professional, and nurses are no exception. Nurse Keith gives you all of the best tips and tools you'll need in this step-by-step guide to empower you to better networking, collaboration, and growth for your career. He's the expert!"

—**Marsha Battee**, RN, Lifestyle Design Strategist for Nurses, Founder of TheBossyNurse.com, RNGetaways.com, and Wealth & Wellness LIVE

"As a referral marketing expert, I can attest to the importance of networking. Keith has written an informative overview filled with good do's and don'ts to maximize your efforts. Adding just a few of these suggestions will increase your success."

—**Susanne Kennedy**, Referral Marketing Expert, Author of the forthcoming book, *Networking for Introverts* www.referralinstitutesantafe.com

"In this time of transition for nurses, Keith Carlson is a stabilizing force offering hope and direction. His networking primer suggests ways in which nurses can grow professionally while supporting and encouraging each other. A must read!"

—**Carol Gino**, RN, MA, CarolGino.com, Bestselling author of *The Nurse's Story*

"Useful, timely, and chock full of realistic strategies that actually work, *Savvy Networking for Nurses* is like learning from a trusted mentor. Keith Carlson does exactly what he teaches in this book—giving everything he can in order to create that deep relationship with the reader. My favorite parts are the personal touch and timely tips he shares throughout each section. A must-read for nurses who are serious about taking their career to the next level."

—**Elizabeth Scala,** MSN/MBA, RN, ElizabethScala.com,
Bestselling author of *Nursing from Within*

Savvy  Networking for Nurses

Getting Connected

(and Staying Connected)

in the 21ST Century

Keith Carlson

RN, BSN, NC-BC

REVISED EDITION
With Updated Linkedin
Information

Nurse Keith
Coaching

Santa Fe, New Mexico

NURSE KEITH CAREER MASTERY SERIES

Published by: Nurse Keith Coaching
            57 Calle Francisca
            Santa Fe, NM, 87507-0150
            NurseKeith.com

Editors: Jeffrey Braucher, Mary Rives
Book design and production: Ann Lowe

Printed in the United States of America

Publisher's Cataloging-in-Publication

Carlson, Keith, 1964- author.
    Savvy networking for nurses : getting connected (and staying connected) in the 21st century / Keith Carlson, RN, BSN, NC-BC.

    pages cm. -- (Nurse Keith career mastery series ; 1)

    1. Nursing--Vocational guidance. 2. Business networks.   I. Title. II. Series: Carlson, Keith, 1964- Nurse Keith career mastery series ; 1.

RT82.C289 2015   610.7306'9
                          QBI15-600190

This book is dedicated to you, the professional nurse, whose tireless work in an incredible variety of settings keeps the engines of health care and wellness running. Whether you're a bedside nurse, nursing student, researcher, educator, nurse manager, administrator, nurse entrepreneur, or retiree, your "nurseness" makes you a member of an elite group of human beings, and I tip my (invisible) nurse's cap in your honor.

Contents

Acknowledgments and Gratitude

I T'S BEEN SAID BEFORE, but no one writes a book alone. I've been encouraged to write a book for quite some time, and despite my many years of professional blogging and freelance writing, a book has simply not manifested until now.

I must express immense gratitude to my wife, Mary Rives—writer, coach, "companion editor" to elders, and therapeutic monologue performer and facilitator—whose support, encouragement, and love have buoyed me for more than a quarter of a century. Mary, you're my world.

For my son, Rene Rives, and my daughter-in-law, Bevin Shagoury; thank you for being such stellar human beings who I hold in my heart of hearts.

I must thank my business partner, friend, and intrepid podcast cohost, Kevin Ross. Kevin is a man of vision, talent, style, deep business acumen, and great heart. He has encouraged and cajoled me for years. Thanks, man!

Many thanks to Phoenix Rising, my local BNI chapter here in Santa Fe, New Mexico. What a supportive, kind, and giving group of like-minded professionals. Givers gain!

Deep thanks to my preliminary readers for their invaluable feedback and advice: Marsha Battee, Susanne Kennedy, Carol Gino, Mary Rives, Kevin Ross, Elizabeth Scala, Beth Boynton, and Renee Thompson.

Sincere gratitude to my fantastic proofreader and editor, Jeffrey Braucher, "The Santa Fe Word Doctor." Jeffrey, your skills have been invaluable to me, and you certainly put the "L" back in public!

Smiles and thanks to Ann Lowe, Santa Fe-based book designer extraordinaire! Thank you so much, Ann. You're the best!

My friend and fellow nurse entrepreneur, Renee Thompson, deserves a great deal of credit for lighting the fire under me when it came to writing a book. Renee, you're a nursing hero, and a dear friend.

Special thanks to Mary Hoggard, a dear friend who truly embodies generosity of spirit and unconditional support.

Deep appreciation to Mercedes Clemens, my stellar nursing colleague and friend. Thank you for being a wonderful person, a fantastic nurse, and my go-to friend for tech questions!

A deep bow to my colleagues at Mi Casa Home Health Care in Albuquerque, NM. Thanks for who you are and what you do!

My thanks to Sarah Santacroce for her breadth of knowledge and expertise regarding LinkedIn and social media.

Other nurse entrepreneurs and thought leaders have also influenced me greatly, including the incomparable Donna Cardillo, the holistic nurse visionaries Linda Bark and Barbie Dossey, and other awe-inspiring nurses upon whose shoulders I stand, or by whose sides I walk.

My immense gratitude also goes to you, my beloved reader. Thank you from the bottom of my nurse's heart.

Preface for the 2nd Edition

WHEN I FIRST PUBLISHED Savvy Networking for Nurses in 2015, I was an outspoken evangelist of the importance of networking for nurses to further their careers, and that hasn't changed in any way. Networking is still at the heart of my career development strategy.

If you met a nurse who changed your life and convinced you that the profession was your calling, that person is part of your network if you chose to stay in touch. If your mother's best friend is the Director of Nursing of an assisted living facility in your hometown, she can be part of your network too. Maybe your insurance agent knows a nurse you'd like to meet, or maybe your IT consultant has connections at the local hospital. They're all potential additions to your network, and they're like gold for your career development and networking strategy.

If you're just starting out in nursing school, you can begin networking on the day you nervously sit down in your first class. Those other students may be as nervous as you, but they're also now your professional peers and colleagues. In fact, you'll share clinical rotations, group projects, and perhaps even work together once you've graduated and entered the workforce. One of your nursing school peers may be your supervisor or charge nurse someday, so it's smart to practice creating positive, lasting relationships with like-minded colleagues. This same principle can apply to veteran nurses attending a continuing education seminar or conference – it's always important and prudent to network throughout your career.

As an expert career coach for 21st-century nurses, my goal is to inspire nurses to elevate themselves and their professional lives through savvy career management and the use of practical tools to get them where they want to go.

This book was born from my desire to reach as many nurses as possible with the simple message that networking is a learned skill, and we can all apply it to move our professional lives along a positive trajectory manifested through conscious intention and forward thinking.

This second edition includes important updated information about LinkedIn. Microsoft bought the platform in 2016, so changes have been rolling out ever since. Be forewarned that LinkedIn is still being tweaked and changed by its new owners, so some of the information in this book may be out of date sometime in the future.

Savvy Networking for Nurses offers insights and inspiration for any nurse who wants to take his or her professional networking to the next level. It will pique your curiosity, challenge you to try your hand at new networking skills, and cajole you to make networking a consistent, constructive, and ultimately enjoyable practice that will manifest countless benefits for your professional career and personal satisfaction.

We can all utilize networking to move
our professional lives in a positive direction
along a trajectory manifested through conscious
intention and forward thinking.

Foreword

ARE YOU PLUGGED IN? Now, let me preface that by saying I'm not asking about plugging in to power up your electronic devices or connect to the Internet, although you will discover that these steps will be important for your online social networking efforts.

I'm actually talking about being plugged into your professional network, connected to those individuals surrounding you every day, and the ones that you should be surrounding yourself with for your own personal and professional growth.

I've often heard from other professionals that they apparently know all the people they're going to need to know in their careers; they've been there and done that. The conversation usually starts with, "I got to where I am today by networking, so I'm all set."

And of course my response is something along the lines of, "Yes, that's great that you've embraced networking to get to where you are right now, but do you think the networking you used to do will get you to where you're going next?"

Usually, the conversation pauses there because I've either stumped this person, or I helped them start a conversation about networking being an ongoing endeavor that you continue to hone over time.

Here's why you made the right choice by taking the first step in reading this book, *Savvy Networking For Nurses*: networking is a teachable skill; it really is. You've also taken a great step forward by going on this journey with Keith Carlson, because I speak from experience when I say that if there's a teachable moment in your career, Keith is going to help guide you there. He truly has a gift to distill the information you need in order to find success.

You will learn how to get started on your networking adventure, how to connect more authentically and deeply, and how to avoid those vacuous connections that really don't offer you (or the other individual) anything meaningful.

Let me take a moment to share a very real situation that happened to me as a CEO. This was a situation in which I was on the receiving end of a networking opportunity that was adroitly orchestrated by an individual who literally took her hustle to a level that got my attention. Now before this story unfolds, let me reiterate that this book and this connection with Keith will help you build these very skills.

Although the approach doesn't always have to go to the level I'm about to share, I will say that if you truly want something different out of your career, whatever it is, then I encourage you to listen to what I'm sharing and what Keith is sharing with you throughout your journey together.

As an entrepreneur with so many endeavors going on at once, so many balls in the air, and ultimately so many aspects of my day-to-day vying for my attention, I am often-times spread razor thin. I do take every opportunity to give as much of my attention to my tasks and the people who need my input when they need it, but it doesn't come easily, and my calendar is often booked months in advance, especially for new connections.

Now, in this particular case that I'm sharing with you, I did have someone reach out to me in a very meaningful way. She took the time to look through all my online profiles, she asked around about what it was like to work with me, and she poured herself into really getting to "know" me, without actually speaking to me or meeting me in person.

After finding out more about who I am as a person, she then figured out how to get in touch with me, and she offered either to hit the trails on our mountain bikes during one of my planned rides, or to buy me a meal at one of my favorite restaurants that she discovered on my Twitter feed. She was relentless regarding having an opportunity to meet with me. She really wanted my attention no matter the setting, and she got it.

Many of you might be thinking that this is really extreme, but it worked for her. This individual is now on one of my teams, and it was one of the best decisions I've ever made, because the hustle and drive she demonstrated in trying to learn about me and meet me continue in her performance for my company.

Again, you don't have to take it to the level I just described, but Keith can help you get there if you so choose. He will also teach you that authentic and meaningful connections are of paramount importance, even during brief and spontaneous encounters.

Change is a constant in networking, but you will continue to hone those skills and pivot your thinking and approach. You will build those connections that will get you beyond where you are now, and take you where you want to end up.

Now go and connect with Keith Carlson by devouring this book. You'll be so glad you did.

– Kevin Ross, RN, BSN
Entrepreneur, Investor, Speaker, and Nurse
CEO and Founder of Spire Health Partners, Inc.
Founder of InnovativeNurse.com and The Innovative Nurse
Show podcast, Co-Host and Founder at RNFM Radio
Champion of out-of-the-box thinking

In the highly connected 21st century, it is
absolutely imperative for savvy professionals to
understand how to build a robust professional
network in the interest of their career.

Introduction

IN THE HIGHLY CONNECTED 21st century, it is absolutely imperative for conscientious and intelligent professionals to understand how to build a robust professional network in the interest of their career. Networking needs to be an intrinsic part of every professional's career-building strategy, and this pertains as much to nurses as it does to lawyers, photographers, CPAs, insurance brokers, and most any other professional you may encounter.

As a professional with a career to manage and develop, you need other professionals in your proverbial corner, and networking—both online and face-to-face—is one of the most powerful vehicles you can employ on a daily basis vis-à-vis the manifestation of your optimal career trajectory.

For an active professional in any industry, networking assists you in creating a tribe of like-minded people you can turn to when you need a recommendation, an informational interview, an introduction, a foot in the door of a specific organization, or a sounding board for your plans and ideas. Your professional network is like a gold mine that can readily yield crucial benefits for your career, and its importance cannot be overstated.

Networking isn't something that you do from time to time; it's an ongoing process that dynamically and organically increases your influence, aligns you with like-minded professionals, and expands your world beyond the confines of your immediate personal sphere.

Smart networking needs to be part of your lifestyle and workstyle as a central aspect of how you move in the world. It's not just about being able to find a job; it's about amassing a tribe of contacts and connections, and creating long-term relationships built upon symbiotic authenticity and positive mutual regard.

Back in the day, one could easily rely on classified ads and online job boards as the sole provider of employment opportunities, but that is certainly changing faster than we can imagine. Having said that, as recently as 2010 I landed two jobs via Craigslist, and I'm currently the Chief Nursing Officer at one of those agencies, so I'm not saying it's impossible. Sure, plenty of employers may still post positions on their websites, as well as on third-party sites like Monster, Glassdoor, and Craigslist. Ads notwithstanding, it behooves every nurse in search of employment to implement a multi-pronged approach to finding work and building their career, and that includes networking.

For better or worse, the world has indeed experienced a massive sea change, and a large number of professional positions are now found through "side door" opportunities, through the people you know and their professional network. Interested colleagues and associates can move your career forward in a way that old-school employment ads simply cannot match. Networking is a powerful tool that will put many of the right people in your corner, for both the short- and long-term well-being of your nursing career.

The advice in this book applies to you, no matter where you are on your career path. Whether you're a nurse working in a clinical position, or a nurse entrepreneur completely removed from bedside care, the need for networking remains the same.

As a career coach, I hear a plethora of reasons why nurses perceive barriers and challenges to networking and building relationships in the interest of their career:

- *"I don't have time to network."*
- *"I'm shy."*
- *"I'm happy at my job. Why should I network?"*
- *"I have nothing to sell. Why is networking important for me?"*
- *"I hate to feel like I'm selling myself."*
- *"I just can't network. It doesn't feel authentic."*

These and other reasons simply aren't strong enough arguments, and those perceived barriers are perceptions, not the reality on the ground. If you're shy, networking online is a great way to break the ice with very little risk, warming you up to the notion of face-to-face networking. If you think you don't have time, you can make time if it's important enough for you to do so.

My friends, I don't mean to frighten you, but the sad reality is that the job you love so much could be downsized at any time. No matter how loyal you are, and no matter how much you're respected by your colleagues, your workplace could declare bankruptcy, be cannibalized by a larger corporation, or simply shut its doors tomorrow. It's a harsh world out there in the 21st-century healthcare landscape, so who you know can be crucial in terms of the robustness, solidity, and longevity of your career.

It is entirely in your best interest to imbue your professional relationships and networking with as much sincerity as possible. The symbiosis and sharing should start with you, so being a giver will ultimately serve you much more than being a person who's always trying to ascertain what others can do for you. (I call such people "networking vultures," and it's something you surely don't want to be.)

For introverted professionals who are relatively averse to face-to-face interaction, online networking will be more of a natural fit. And for those who are technophobic or lacking in computer skills, face-to-face may be easier. However, for those of you who eschew both the computer and face-to-face worlds, you have some decisions to make—and some skills to learn.

Givers get much further in this life, so be a consistent giver and you can't go wrong. Bear in mind that those you give to may not give back to you directly per se, but what goes around comes around, and your generosity of spirit will never be a waste of time or energy.

From the intelligent use of LinkedIn, Twitter, Facebook, and other social media platforms, to understanding how to engage in effective face-to-face networking, and so on, learning the skills of creating connection, building rapport, and sustaining relationships is key to your professional success and happiness.

This small volume is packed with useful information; it offers the earnest healthcare professional the means by which he or she can up their game when it comes to networking, and take meaningful and powerful steps in the direction of creating a more authentic and well-rounded network of professional contacts.

Throughout the book, you will find highlighted quotes that are meant to inspire you to reflect on various aspects of networking. You will also find sections titled "Inspired Action," where you are encouraged to take action to improve your networking habits and skills. There are also several blank pages for your own notes and thoughts at the back of the book.

I want to inspire you to take a long, serious look at your current network, assess your networking strategy (if you have one), and then take bold steps toward moving your networking to the next level—even if that means starting to network because you've never done so before.

Whether you're a novice nurse just out of school, a nurse entrepreneur, a mid-career nurse seeking to advance your career in a new and exciting direction, or a retiring nurse seeking a post-retirement trajectory, this book will guide you in developing a powerful strategy that will embolden and energize your career path for years to come.

Thank you for joining me on this journey. I hope you'll get in touch as you implement these tips and tricks in the interest of a happy and satisfying professional life, and a solid professional network.

Cheers!

–Nurse Keith

Because the 21st-century world is so highly
connected, I invite you to consider how
relationships can be the veritable backbone
of your professional life.

CHAPTER 1

My Story

I COME FROM A JEWISH FAMILY of Eastern European and Russian heritage, and I find that most Jewish people are quite naturally oriented toward a sense of tribe, family, collectivism, and belonging. I have always been a relational person; throughout my life, my sense of self has admittedly been strongly and irrevocably formed from my relationships with others.

As a teenager, I was determined to attend art school. With a number of relatively well-known (and some very well-known) musicians and artists on my mother's side of the family, the die was cast, and I attended (and summarily dropped out of) two art schools in Philadelphia.

Although I enjoyed the camaraderie of all-nighters in the printmaking studio, and the outsider persona we all worked so hard to develop as art students in the post-punk early 1980s, the solitary nature of making art was not for me. Although I briefly entertained the notion of pursuing art therapy as a course of study, that discipline still seemed quite esoteric in 1984, and I decided to leave school and enter the big wide world as a college dropout.

In the aftermath of art school and a 12-month hitchhiking trip around Europe (which included living briefly on a collective kibbutz in Israel), I subsequently became a massage therapist, yoga teacher, husband, and stepfather by the time I reached my 25th birthday. I found myself drawn more and more naturally into the helping professions, and it seems that the path continued to open up before me, no matter what I did or didn't do.

While attempting to grow my massage and yoga practices with little to no business acumen, I engaged in working as a caregiver and personal care attendant with many populations, including the developmentally disabled, the elderly, and people with HIV/AIDS. I loved this type of work, and I soon realized that it was the relationships that were central to the deep satisfaction experienced in everything I did. The mastery of skills was fine, but the mastery of communication and emotional caregiving was paramount.

Approaching my 30th birthday, I was spontaneously struck with the notion that, as a father with a prepubescent son, I needed a remunerative and flexible career that would propel me through the next several decades of parenting and saving for our future. Having eschewed the artistic lifestyles of my maternal ancestors, I realized there were three nurses on my father's side of the family, and suddenly nursing became the vehicle by which I felt I could achieve personal and professional satisfaction, coupled with admirable earning potential as a young parent and husband.

During this time I thought deeply about my Aunt Sylvia and her life partner, Jan. They were long-time nurses, and Jan used to regale us with stories of being a nurse to General George Patton during World War II. I never knew if her tales were true or not, but they obviously struck a chord with me, lodging themselves deep within my impressionable young psyche. Jan would repeatedly tell stories of ordering Patton to soak his painful hemorrhoids in his helmet out on the battlefield, so I frequently say that I owe a debt of gratitude to Patton's hindquarters for my choosing to become a nurse. (I also have an understandable preference for sitz baths, rather than helmets.)

Nursing school and my clinical rotations were revelatory for me, and I took to nursing like a duck to water. The relational aspects of nursing came naturally, and I found that my gifts for relationship, communication, and emotional intelligence were a perfect fit for my chosen career path. I excelled in school, and when I graduated I embarked on a career that has continued to bring me great contentment, both personally and professionally.

Fourteen or fifteen years into my nursing career, I discovered the emerging field of coaching, thanks to my wife's consistent exploration of new and unique modalities. Through trial, error, and finding the right resources at just the right time, I discovered that nurses were the people I wanted to work and play with as a coach. I was truly inspired to help nurses live happier and healthier lives, and this desire eventually manifested in a wonderful practice focusing on holistic career coaching for smart nurses like you, and the achievement of becoming a Board Certified Nurse Coach (NC-BC) through the American Holistic Nurses Credentialing Corporation (AHNCC).

My nursing career has been built on a foundation of networking, even though I hadn't even realized that networking was a practice that came naturally to me. Connection, collaboration, and authenticity have been the hallmarks of my career and the relationships within it, and I am now fired up to inspire other nurses to learn how networking can assist them in manifesting more of what they want in their careers and lives.

As a working nurse, holistic career coach, social media expert, freelance writer, well-known nurse blogger, and successful podcaster, I bring a great deal of experience to my coaching practice. It is my personal mission to inspire and educate other nurses and healthcare professionals to realize the power of relationships built upon authentic connection and mutuality.

Because the 21st-century world is so highly connected, I invite you to consider how relationships can be the true backbone of your professional life.

Like I said, I come from a Jewish background where relationships and connectivity are central to the culture, informing and underpinning our individual and collective *raison d'etre*. When you read this book, you're in relationship with a part of me that I've poured into these pages, and I treasure the notion that we're now connected through the printed word, a love of nursing, and a desire for deeper relationships and increased satisfaction in our personal and professional lives.

INSPIRED THOUGHT

What personal experiences, memories, family members, or values have influenced your career choices and the work you've chosen to do in the world?

Your network is a tapestry, a web of
interconnected and potentially interdependent
individuals who represent an enormous
brain trust of skill, expertise, and deeply
held knowledge.

CHAPTER 2

How to Network and Why

THERE'S A LOT OF TALK about the importance of networking and professional relationships. Why do so many people think it's paramount to build positive relationships on behalf of their career or business? Let's take a look at some of the most salient reasons.

Collective Genius

One day I was discussing the importance of networking with a career-coaching client who happened to be a nurse. I mentioned the notion that the power of your professional and personal network is a form of collective genius that can be tapped when you need it most. That idea still resonates to this day.

We've all heard of geniuses like Albert Einstein, Marie Curie, Stephen Hawking, and Simone de Beauvoir. And yet many of us are geniuses in our own right, whether it be the commonly thought of genius that manifests intellectually, or one that manifests emotionally, spiritually, relationally, or otherwise.

> ## INSPIRED THOUGHT
>
> What forms of genius do *you* embody? Don't be
> shy; admit it to yourself! No one's watching!

Collective genius is something altogether different from individual genius. When considering how to create a community of friends and colleagues you can co-create true symbiotic relationships with, your network is the place to begin that exciting and powerful process.

Your network is a tapestry, a web of interconnected and potentially interdependent individuals who represent an enormous brain trust of skill, expertise, and deeply held knowledge. As a professional with the goal of success and forward movement in your career, it's incumbent upon you to create lasting relationships with mutual advancement in mind. Some of these relationships may turn into valuable, deep friendships, and others will remain strictly businesslike. These relationships are intrinsic particles within your personal universe.

When you're looking for a job, moving to another region of the country, starting a business, creating a product, returning to school, or attempting to begin research for some aspect of your career, your network is the first place to turn for expert support, cogent feedback, or creative ideas. That brain trust is truly only a keystroke or phone call away, and you can reach out at any time, requesting input or suggestions when you're ready to receive such invaluable responses and advice.

When I was working on the first draft of this book, I looked to the many stars within the firmament of my personal network, asking them to read, review, and comment on the first or second drafts. Their feedback was essential to the formation of the book you're now reading, and when I think about it, I met almost every one of those amazing individuals through networking, whether online or otherwise. It's a wonderful thing, and I'm ever so grateful to those members of my network who contributed to the successful completion of this book, most of whom I would not have met without assiduously networking over the years.

Networking and Mutuality

Did you notice I mentioned *"mutual advancement"* in one of the preceding paragraphs when describing the ultimate goals of your networking endeavors? That's because mutuality is the key to networking. When you bring someone into your network and they become a member of your personal brain trust, guess what? You're also a member of *their* brain trust! That mutual mindset is important, since being a giving person is one of the keys to fully receiving. After all, in the end, givers receive more than takers, don't they?

Symbiotic professional relationships are indeed the name of the game. Give and take, mutual support, giving without expecting anything in return, and being present for your colleagues when they need you is the *modus operandi* for you to fully internalize and personify throughout your career. The members of my network who gave of their time to help shape this book have given beautifully and generously to me, and I'm always wondering how I can give back to those who have stood by my side (or allowed me to cry on their shoulder).

Remember those "networking vultures" I mentioned earlier? They sadly don't seem to understand these crucial aspects of mutuality, and perhaps they never will. Needless to say, symbiosis and mutual benefit are central to having the ability to effectively build a network that feels authentic and reflects your intention to be a giver, not a taker.

Like they say in the trademarked motto of BNI (Business Network International), "givers gain." This could not be more true for your professional networking and community-building efforts, and if you're a giver and a connector, go for it. However, if you need to up your game around networking and being a giving colleague, today is the day to begin.

Symbiotic professional relationships, connections, and communities are priceless. If you actively and consistently build them with an eye toward a fulfilling present and a successful future, you have so much to gain, as do your lucky connections.

Own Your Network

When I say you need to own your network, I don't mean you "own" people or their ideas. What I would like you to consider is truly embracing the knowledge and collective genius of your network by realizing its power, and choosing to tap that genius at key times in your career. Most of us don't think about the sheer value of our network, but internalizing its value is one of the first steps to knowing that you can utilize it for the advancement of your career and professional trajectory at the most crucial moments that present themselves.

Whether you're a nursing student, a seasoned professional, or in mid-career flux, networking (both in person and online) has never been a more intelligent and timely career development tool. I contend that online and face-to-face networking skills should be developed and maintained throughout your career, and that building a robust professional network is a key to success. Since these skills aren't really taught in school, you simply have to learn them on your own by turning to expert resources for guidance in knowing exactly how to go about it.

When you develop authentic, symbiotic relationships with a growing cohort of like-minded professionals in your industry (as well as industries beyond your niche), you'll be able to tap the expertise and collective genius of that network when you need it most.

Shallow Networking

Before we get to the subject of deep networking, let's start with the shallow kind first, which I believe is the most common form of networking practiced regularly by most people.

- In shallow networking, you create a lackluster *LinkedIn* profile, and you then send random, generically impersonal invitations in order to connect with other people you have no real alignment with or interest in. Meanwhile, you'll likely never follow up after they accept your invitation.

- Shallow networking involves mindlessly "collecting" connections without any plan or strategy to do anything particularly inspiring to follow up or build upon those relationships. The purpose is barely perceptible, and may even be lost on the person doing it.

- In this form of networking, you meet another professional, put their business card in your wallet, and then can't remember who they are or why you saved their card in the first place. Their card gets recycled, and you never see them again—or if you run into them, you don't recognize them or remember how or where you met.

- Using shallow networking, you "work a room" by handing out cards to every person you see.

- In shallow networking, you think about what others can do for you, and nothing else. You focus on what you can get—like a networking vulture. And in a room full of networking vultures, nobody gets anywhere.

INSPIRED ACTION

List three ways in which you have taken part in shallow networking. How did it work for you, and how could it have been better?

Deep Networking

Deep networking is an entirely different approach. In deep networking you reach out to others with purpose and authenticity; you consistently follow through on your intentions, and you continue the conversation that began when you first met a new contact.

In deep networking, you create long-lasting, authentic connections that deepen and ripen with time and consistent commitment. There's no rush, but there is indeed a true desire for the establishment of a bond, to whatever extent that that bond naturally develops. You can't force it to happen, but you can fan the flames of close association conscientiously and purposefully.

More than just trying to figure out what others can do for you, deep networking means you consistently keep the people within your network "top of mind," and you actively seek ways to assist your colleagues in advancing their professional success and aspirations.

In my local chapter of BNI (Business Network International), my fellow chapter members and I meet every week, and we continue to educate one another about the referrals we're looking for, the types of people we want to meet, the connections we need in order to move forward in our careers or businesses, and how we would like the other members to help us in that regard. Most of us meet one-on-one to further these conversations, and I truly enjoy the ongoing, growing rapport that develops with members of the chapter. We deepen our relationships over time, as well as our understanding of one another as human beings and dedicated professionals, and it's this common vision that feeds those valuable connections.

Deep networking means that relationships are paramount, and you revel in your ability to introduce like-minded colleagues to one another, nurture symbiotic relationships, forge alliances and professional collaborations, and otherwise support those professionals who you trust, admire, and respect.

INSPIRED ACTION

Name three occasions in which you took part in deep networking. What was special about it? What was the outcome?

This type of networking takes diligence and thoughtful action, as well as a true desire to build a network not only for your own benefit, but also for the benefit of others. Again, symbiosis is key.

Networking as Art

Deep networking transmutes the "work" of networking into a playful, life-enhancing activity that can be likened to an art form. The art of networking is a human art, one born of a creative impulse and an honest motivation for positive associations and mutuality.

As an artful networker, you weave a tapestry of collaboration and good will that has the power to transform otherwise humdrum acquaintances into enriching partnerships.

The art of networking can be nurtured through:

- Thoughtful actions that create new opportunities for your colleagues and connections.
- Honing your communication skills over the course of your career in the interest of improving your ability to connect with others.
- Seeing networking as an art form that you can practice, improve upon, and lend your own personal flair and personality.
- Creatively approaching your network as an organic masterpiece that will never be finished, but that nonetheless deserves your utmost attention and care for the long haul.
- Consistently giving to others in increasingly generous ways.

INSPIRED THOUGHT

How could you bring more artfulness to your networking endeavors? How could you creatively expand your network or take inspired action for the benefit of some of your most valued connections?

Build It Thoughtfully

Those who network in pursuit of depth thoughtfully seek connections that have meaning and potential. While it's true that not every connection can be a deep one, the deep networker is always on the lookout for ways to enhance current relationships and enrich their own life—and the lives of others—through forging still more high-quality relationships.

Of course, when you have 750 connections on LinkedIn, you obviously can't hop on the phone or Skype with every single person, so it's only natural that some people won't have a very personal relationship with you. Just like on your personal Facebook page, there are bound to be people you don't know very well; this is normal and expected on social media in the 21st century. We'll discuss LinkedIn and social media in more detail later in this book.

INSPIRED ACTION

Who are six of your most valued professional
connections? What makes them so valuable?

If you focus on just some of your professional relationships, nurture them, and generate a creative symbiosis with
select members of your network, you're well on your way to
a deeper place in your networking efforts, and greater results
for yourself and your colleagues.

For example, several years ago, I met Sarah Santacroce, a
well-known Swiss entrepreneur, on LinkedIn. Since Sarah is
a LinkedIn expert, I hired her to assist me with increasing my
understanding of the breadth and depth of the platform. Over
time, we've become friendly colleagues, she has appeared several times as a guest on RNFM Radio, our podcast for nurses,
and she and I are frequently in touch. Sarah and I have created a
mutually beneficial and fruitful relationship, and we continue
to find ways to collaborate and support each other. This is
only one example of how relationships on LinkedIn and other
social media platforms can develop and deepen over time.

INSPIRED ACTION

List three connections on LinkedIn you would like to deepen your relationship with, along with a deadline for reaching out to them.

Deep networking isn't about going deep with everyone; it's about seeking increased depth with the professionals you feel the most resonance with. Deep networking is moving beyond the superficial, and doing it in the spirit of collaboration, cooperation, and partnership.

Networking can be fun, enlivening, purposeful, authentic, and creative, and every relationship has its own purpose and flavor. That said, the actual purpose of the connection may very well not emerge for some time, so if you can let go of any attachment to outcome, you're likely to relax into the relationship for its own sake, and simply await the blossoming of your budding professional kinship.

Go deep when you can, share your story, elicit the stories of others, build relationships, and be authentic. When you network in search of depth, you swim with the friendly, mutually minded school, not with the sharks of narcissism, who are apparently in cahoots with the networking vultures flying overhead.

Building Rapport

Building rapport with other professionals can only truly be achieved through real relationships over time, whether those individuals are potential clients, referral partners, or like-minded colleagues.

Sure, connecting on LinkedIn with another interesting professional is helpful, but isn't it even more productive and meaningful to actually have a conversation with that person, building on the original online acquaintance? You obviously can't make a personal connection with every person you meet on LinkedIn or other social media platforms, but you can choose some individuals with whom you feel a professional or personal alignment, and pursue deeper relationships accordingly.

In professional relationships within your local area, there's nothing like chatting over coffee or breaking bread together to cement a real connection that can potentially reap myriad rewards and outcomes. Some of my business and networking connections have developed into deep, lifelong friendships, fruitful business partnerships, referral partners, and professional associations that have been empowering, fun, satisfying, and supportive. And, like I said, some of those people indeed read and commented on the very book you're holding in your hands. How cool is that?

Building Community

Whether you're building community around a brand, service, or product, or you're creating a deep network in support of your nursing career, amassing an effective and proactive army of people who respect and support you is a very intelligent professional strategy. This is an army whose sole mission is creating symbiotic mutual support, and it can be a very powerful army indeed.

Your professional community may consist of these and other categories of supportive individuals:

- Like-minded nursing colleagues
- Satisfied customers or clients
- Professionals in other industries
- Current and former professors or teachers
- Current and former colleagues
- Sympathetic and interested neighbors
- Family members and friends who are aligned with your professional and career aspirations
- Anyone you feel aligned with, personally or professionally

INSPIRED ACTION

List four people from the above list of categories who you can proactively bring into your professional community, and a deadline for when you will contact them.

Build for the Future

A professional community or network doesn't need to live in the same area, and they don't all need to know one another. Your network is a tapestry of individuals or groups who understand and appreciate who you are, what you do, and what you're all about (to whatever degree they're willing and able to do so). Some networks are loose, some are tightly knit, but most are a fascinating combination of the two.

Even if you're happy in your current position and have no desire for change, you must understand that change in your career or workstyle may someday be thrust upon you. No matter how happy you may be in your career, if your dream job comes along and you feel compelled to pursue that golden opportunity, it's reassuring and comforting to have a stable of reliable, intelligent professionals in your network. These are individuals you can turn to for support in your endeavors, and they can also benefit from your friendship, kindness, and expertise.

Types of Networkers

There are various types of negative networkers. Other than mentioning the ubiquitous networking vultures, energy vampires, and the folks who mindlessly press a business card into every hand they see, I won't try to describe the many types of unskilled networkers that are lurking out there at so many events and meetings. I suggest we focus on the positive.

I have met some consummate networkers in my day, and many of them are in my various circles of influence. Off the top of my head I can name at least five people who are almost flawless in their networking skills and practices. These people dress up, show up, follow up, connect, listen, and then listen some more. They're superstars in my digital Rolodex.

If you Google "types of networkers," there are a great many lists developed by various writers, experts, and thought leaders. I've taken the opportunity to conjure up my own four archetypes for your edification. Like any system of archetypes, most people don't fit just one; you may see aspects of yourself or people you know in many or all of these, and that's fine. At different times, we all embody and manifest various skills and attributes, and we can choose to develop and strengthen the aspects that will serve us best.

Personally, I straddle several networking archetypes. I'm generally fairly gregarious and extroverted in most circumstances at this point in my life, but I also have times when my introverted nature is more prevalent. So, if I'm attending a networking event or conference during a period of time when my introverted nature has come to the fore, I can fake it and force myself to reach out, or I can hang back and try to connect with one special person, not thirty. It's a dance, and we make our own steps in the moment.

So, my friends, here's my list of the four main types of skilled, positive networkers I have observed in action:

The Connector

Connectors are all about connecting their colleagues with one another. Connectors see potential in the coming together of various individuals or groups, and they skillfully plan and coordinate so that like-minded friends or colleagues can meet, interact, and potentially collaborate. These types of networkers keep their contacts top of mind, and they're excellent at seeing the 10,000-foot view of how one person meeting another could result in positive outcomes.

The Connector will set up a conference call, send an introductory email to various parties in order to start a conversation, or invite three colleagues to meet him or her for a lunchtime meet and greet. Once the conversation gets going, they sit back and enjoy, but they can also, if need be, skillfully facilitate the conversation in positive and interesting directions that honor each person at the table. The Connector thrives on connecting people to one another, and generally asks for nothing in return.

The Pollinator

Pollinators like to sprinkle their networking dust where it will most readily have a beneficial impact. Pollinators may not introduce individuals to one another as readily as Connectors; rather, they empower and cajole particular individuals to fulfill their potential by urging them out into a particular sphere or world. The Pollinator will give a colleague a VIP invitation to a big networking event, and explain how attending may be very beneficial for that individual. Pollinators are like networking Fairy Godmothers, and they are thrilled when their seeds of empowerment result in blossoming success.

The Collaborator

Collaborators rarely miss an opportunity to consider how they might collaborate with a connection in order to build a process or endeavor that will result in a mutually beneficial outcome. When they're talking to a colleague or connection, their mind is in overdrive, considering various ways in which this connection could result in a mutually beneficial collaborative effort.

Collaborators are community-minded; they like to roll up their sleeves, put on their thinking caps, and match wits and share ideas with colleagues who are equally excited about collaborative ventures and the magic they can create.

The Quiet Networker

The Quiet Networker is less out front than the others, but no less effective. He or she is more of a wallflower at big events, and prefers quiet, one-on-one meetings that can be examined from the peace of his or her own mind and heart. Quiet Networkers may not be as exciting or dynamic on the outside, but they're deep thinkers who consider their networking very carefully, and love the depth of connection that comes with forethought and measured action. They're the networking Tortoise to the Connector's Hare.

Which of these four networking archetypes most fits your personality as a networker, or are there two or three in which you see yourself? (I actually see myself in all four!)

INSPIRED THOUGHT

If there were one networker archetype you would most like to develop in yourself in the next year, which one would it be, and why? Now, take inspired action and develop that archetype with intention!

When you're networking, your
personal brand is what people
experience and respond to.

CHAPTER 3

Your Personal Brand

I N A BOOK ABOUT PROFESSIONAL networking, you may be surprised to find a section on personal branding. Please indulge me and understand that I'm including personal branding because it's fundamentally intrinsic to your networking strategy as a 21st-century professional. Believe me, your personal brand needs and deserves your attention, and perhaps one of my subsequent books will focus even more deeply on the practice and art of personal branding.

Brands Abound

We all readily recognize brands in the marketplace without much thought. Patagonia, Apple, Ben and Jerry's, Newman's Own, T-Mobile—these brands want us to think of them in a specific way, and they present a particular image of themselves through advertisements and other media as they compete for our attention, loyalty, and ultimately, our money.

Brands can conjure many feelings, including nostalgia, hope, dread, joy, mistrust, relaxation, adventure, and prosperity. For example, Aflac's duck mascot can make us smile, but for some of us, Monsanto's commercials about their genetically modified seeds incite us to throw things at the TV.

Our reactions to these brands occur based on a variety of personal beliefs, values, and experiences, and some of our reactions may be quite visceral (and possibly entirely subconscious). Branding is powerful stuff, and many people earn a great deal of money because of the allure and influence of brands.

The concept of personal branding may somehow feel manipulative to the uninitiated. You may think about the ways you've felt misled or deceived by corporate brands you previously admired, trusted, or patronized, and this is understandable.

For example, perhaps you loved Ben and Jerry's because they represented hippie values being leveraged into a high-quality, fun product that subsequently infiltrated the mainstream. Sadly, you then learn that Ben and Jerry sold out to Unilever, the massive Anglo-Dutch conglomerate, and your previous admiration for their slightly outsider stance adjusts to a cynical realization that even hippies can choose to squelch some of their core values in the interest of business. In your universe, that brand just lost some of its sheen. (But you may still find Chunky Monkey veritably irresistible.)

INSPIRED THOUGHT

What are three brands you have positive regard for? Why do you feel positive about them? What do they convey that inspires confidence, loyalty, or affectionate regard?

So, you may ask, what does branding have to do with you, the professional nurse? My response would be this: "Pretty much everything."

Do You Have a Brand?

Whether you like it or not, you have a personal brand. Honest. You may not think about it much, but you do. And if the term "brand" just turns your stomach into queasy knots of undigested lunch, try substituting "persona" in place of "brand," and see if your lunch settles more easily.

For my part, I want you to consider adjusting to the use of this term, which is usually associated only with companies, so I'm going to keep using it. Sorry, but let's consider this "Personal Branding Desensitization 101." Don't worry; it'll be okay.

The Fear of Self-Commodification

For those who consider branding a dirty word that conjures images of commercial brands they find questionable, creating an idealized aspect of yourself may feel a little false; some might even call it sleazy. I understand this perception; none of us really wants to be turned into a consumable product that's judged on appearance, and that can be what turns some individuals away from the notion of personal branding altogether.

In this contemporary world that often appears to be built on image rather than substance, this idea of branding can seem like a concerted push for every professional to become an object, a commodity that's traded between businesses and employers. This is indeed one perception, but how we approach the notion of our own personal brand is key.

The idea of *impression management* is often used in social psychology, and I would venture that we are all indeed constantly trying to manage the impressions that others have of us. Even as children, we try to look cool, and we choose clothes, lunchboxes, and notebooks that will "brand" us in a certain way. Granted, the culture and society inundate us with commercials and advertisements that tell us what we're supposed to look like and how we're supposed to act, but it may very well be intrinsic to our human nature to want to impress others. Neanderthals probably chose certain skins or weapons (imagine rocks and bones) in order to make an impression on both friends and enemies alike, and ancient Egyptians certainly tried to ensure that their image would be very specifically portrayed in the afterlife. Was King Tut a brand ambassador sent into the future? Tut is branded to the max!

In my book, if your motives are pure and authentic, and you're not trying to manipulate people in a nefarious manner, your efforts at personal branding safely fall within the realm of normal human impression management.

Creating Your Personal Brand

When you're actively networking, your personal brand is what people experience and respond to. In fact, your brand is in action at every moment of the day, no matter who you may be interacting with. However, in your professional life and career, this is where your brand really needs to shine.

During your interactions with colleagues, your tone of voice, demeanor, grooming, manner of dress, level of professionalism, and personality are assessed, considered, and then categorized in the perceiver's brain. They may perceive you negatively, positively, or neutrally, and when questioned, they would likely be able to conjure any number of adjectives to describe you, even if only after a 15-minute meeting. First impressions are indeed powerful, but I believe that subsequent, ongoing impressions are more powerful and memorable. Your brand ultimately manifests in how people feel after experiencing your presence, whether in person or in the virtual world.

INSPIRED THOUGHT

What eight adjectives would your colleagues use to describe your professional demeanor, appearance, style, and way of being?

The form of personal branding I'm discussing involves exactly what my avowed style of networking entails: authenticity. Yes, you want to be entirely yourself, creating a brand that represents who you are as a person, as a nurse, as a healthcare professional, as a human being—and as a positive, contributing citizen of the world.

If you want to project a certain image and persona as a healthcare professional and nurse, consider what you want the perceiver to experience about you. What is the authentic "you" that you wish them to perceive? What will be their take away from having met you? This isn't manipulation; it's simply devoting thoughtful consideration to how you are perceived and experienced by others, and then "walking your talk" on a daily basis.

INSPIRED THOUGHT

Name four characteristics that express how you want to be most readily recognized as a professional. Ask yourself if you actively cultivate those characteristics and attributes through your deeds, words, and personal presence.

Your Brand and In-Person Networking

As I stated above, your brand and persona consist of a multitude of factors, many of which you actually exercise a great deal of control over. Such factors are crucial to consider in terms of face-to-face networking.

Food For Thought:

- When attending a business meeting or networking event, how do you dress? What does your physical appearance reflect about you?
- Are you conscious of body language and eye contact? Do others feel "seen" by you?
- Is your handshake perceived as sincere and firm?
- Do your colleagues perceive you as anxious, or calm and collected?
- Do you appear organized and well put together?
- How do your voice and manner of speaking represent who you are?
- Do you listen well? Do you interrupt others in mid-sentence? Do those conversing with you feel heard?
- When you describe your professional work and career, what do others hear in your voice? Are you seen as enthusiastic and positive, or pessimistic, cynical, and unhappy?
- If you're a nurse entrepreneur or businessperson, how do you communicate the essence of what you do, who you are, and what your services and products are?
- When meeting others, are you interested and interesting?
- Do you have a memorable business card in your pocket and hand it out freely to those you meet? Do

you ask for others' cards, and then follow up in a
timely manner?

- How do others feel after spending time with you?

Whether you are attending a local chapter meeting of a
nursing organization, socializing at a Chamber of Commerce
networking event, or interviewing for a professional position,
you are demonstrating the qualities of your personal brand—
your professional persona—at every moment. What could be
more important when building relationships?

Your Online Brand

In contrast to your personal brand in face-to-face networking,
you may find the idea of your online brand easier to digest
and accept. Your personal brand's online presence is a representation of you—sort of your digital doppelganger, if you
will—so this aspect of personal branding may seem closer to
your internalized notion of what a brand is.

As I alluded above, the branding of corporate entities
like Apple has a great deal to do with logos, advertisements,
the glitz and glamour of celebrities, cultural iconography, the
feelings generated by a product or service, and however else
these corporations try to convince us to buy their stuff and
develop long-standing brand loyalty.

For you, the professional nurse, your online brand consists
of anything about you that exists on the Internet, for better or
worse. If you're careful about your online presence, good for

you; it's smart to understand the realities of how your online world can impact your professional life in various ways.

For those of you who are less careful, the woeful aspects of your online presence may be those drunken vacation photos from Mexico, or the embarrassing college photos posted on Facebook by your old friends. Your online brand may also be colored by the snarky comments you post on Twitter regarding your colleagues and patients. I can hear your brain scanning your Facebook profile as you read these words. This isn't about paranoia; it's about brand management, and it's worth your careful consideration.

In the 21st century, many aspects of our lives are now lived online, and you can be sure that many potential colleagues, collaborators, and employers will Google the heck out of you before an interview or meeting. What will they find? Do you even know? Do you want to know?

Some online privacy advocates will say that nothing you delete from an online account is ever really "gone." Those deleted photos may disappear from your Facebook feed, but they still live on an unidentified server somewhere out there in cyberspace. Sure, they may never again see the digital light of day, but I suggest being conscious of the reality that anything you post will live in perpetuity somewhere, and making decisions accordingly. Even the most embarrassing photo that you hurriedly deleted from Facebook the next morning may already have been downloaded onto someone's hard drive, so be thoughtful and circumspect before you send that image or message out into the ether. Face it: once it's online, it's out of your hands.

If you choose to tweet without anonymity, like I and many other professionals do, consider very carefully what messages you're conveying to the world. If your personal Facebook profile is shared publicly, understand that what's on there can potentially be found, seen, and read. You may also choose to "friend" professional colleagues on Facebook, so consider what you want them to know about you and your personal life. Others form their opinions about us based on many aspects of our lives, including how we represent ourselves online.

Although it's a useful adage to live by, you don't just want to consider if your grandmother would want to see what you're posting. (Who knows? She may already be your friend on Facebook!) You may also want to consider if you're totally comfortable with a potential colleague or employer reading your posts. If you're not altogether comfy, think twice before you publish. (And if you need to remember this golden rule, you could try taping a photo of your grandmother and your boss to your computer screen. If that's not enough to help you edit your online presence, I don't know what is.)

As a professional, you can be certain that LinkedIn is one place where many colleagues and employers will purposefully seek you out. Not only do they want to learn where you've worked, they also want to assess how you represent yourself online. Although LinkedIn is much more than an online resume, there are aspects of the platform that are indeed akin to a resume or CV on steroids. You can upload photos, videos, documents, certificates, and projects to your LinkedIn profile, and this online representation of your professional life can speak volumes about you and your career. In the next section of this book, we'll dive deeper into the importance of LinkedIn, so begin considering how you would like this powerful platform to speak for your personal brand.

INSPIRED THOUGHT

What type of presence do you have online? How do you feel about the manner in which you represent yourself in the digital world? Is your online presence authentic and transparent?

Online Branding Is Also About Relationships

As much as face-to-face networking is all about relationships, online networking is also similarly oriented. How you approach your relationships on LinkedIn, Twitter, Facebook, and other virtual platforms says so much about you, and some of these digital relationships can serve you very well over time, with some eventually transforming into face-to-face relationships and friendships. It really does happen.

When cultivating your online brand, use kindness, generosity, humor, and intelligence in your communications. Infuse your relationships with sincerity and personality, and make sure your images, words, and overall online persona are in line with who you are, what you're all about, and how you want the world to perceive and experience you. Complete transparency may not be advisable in all situations, but conscientious, relative transparency is recommended.

One caveat: There are people whose online persona has almost no relationship to who they really are as actual individuals. An online persona can be light years away from the life an individual really lives. We naturally "edit" our day-to-day lives so only aspects of it actually show up online; this is normal and expected. However, we can take that editing so far that our online persona is a grave mismatch in relation to who we are in real life.

Personally, I try to ensure that my online self is an accurate representation of my true, authentic day-to-day self. When I meet an online friend in real life, there's a natural alignment between what they've seen online and what they perceive when they meet me in the flesh.

The online world can be an extension of our three-dimensional world, and one can—and should—enhance the other. In my experience, I've manifested authentic friendships, remunerative and symbiotic business partnerships, as well as wonderful professional relationships through my online life, and some of those relationships have led to phone calls, Skype sessions, and satisfying and fun in-person meetings. There's little separation between my online and face-to-face networking now; they're simply all of a piece, and they serve me very well on myriad levels.

The goal of face-to-face networking is the same as online networking: building an authentic professional network.

CHAPTER 4

Face-to-Face Networking Strategies

THE GOAL OF FACE-TO-FACE networking is the same as online networking: building an authentic professional network. While online networking can be done in your pajamas, face-to-face networking involves dressing up and showing up in person. This can be challenging for some of us, but let's face it, if you're a nursing professional out in the world, meeting people is a necessity.

INSPIRED THOUGHT

The 3 cardinal rules of face-to-face networking are:
Dress up • Show up • Follow up
How can you instill these rules and take your networking to the most polished, professional level possible?

In-person networking occurs in the workplace, at school, as well as at professional conferences, seminars, and meetings. However, aside from these more formal settings, networking can also occur at the grocery store, while pumping gas, chatting with the people at the next table in a restaurant, or while walking your dog.

Now, I'm not saying you should be "on the prowl" for networking opportunities at every moment of your life, but you truly never know when someone you're talking to may be a veritable gold mine of information, contacts, or connections. That person at the next table could be a senator with influence over healthcare policy in your state. And the woman with the sweet pug who's playing with your labradoodle may be the sister of the Director of Nursing at the hospital where you've been dying to work since you graduated from nursing school. See what I mean? You just never know, so assume that everyone you meet is important and worth your time and attention—because they are.

INSPIRED ACTION

Name three places where you regularly spend time
(for either personal or professional reasons), and
where you can take inspired action in terms of
cultivating positive, symbiotic, and authentic
relationships, especially with other professionals.
Set a date for when you will begin keeping this
goal top of mind while you spend time
in these places.

Essential Tools

For face-to-face networking, you'll need a few simple tools
in your career-building toolbox at all times. These tools
make it easier to connect with others, communicate clearly
about yourself and your brand (remember your brand?),
and leave a few breadcrumbs for further follow-up and
engagement.

Your resume

No matter how happily employed you are, you should be
reviewing, editing, and updating your resume every six
months, without fail. It doesn't matter if you never plan to
apply for another job for the rest of your life; your resume
should always be up-to-date and ready to share.

Let's imagine you meet a potentially influential person in
line at the grocery store, and they ask you to send them your

resume right away because they're having breakfast the next morning with someone you'd love to meet. Wouldn't it be so convenient not to have to stay up until 3am tweaking the dusty resume you haven't touched in four years?

If you need reminders, set a date for resume revision in your calendar for every spring and fall when most of us set our clocks an hour forward or backward, and when some people also change the batteries in their smoke alarms. This way, when you change those smoke alarm batteries, you'll also hear an internal alarm reminding you to update you resume and recharge the batteries of your career.

Your basic cover letter

You need to have a basic cover letter and thank-you letter in your computer files so you can adapt them for a specific position or opportunity at a moment's notice. It's also advisable to have the skeleton of a so-nice-to-meet-you letter on file so that the person you chatted with at the grocery store can receive a professional note from you along with your resume.

(Please note: Your cover letters, thank-you letters, and resume should be printed on high-quality resume paper using a laser printer. Make sure that the font, style, spacing, formatting, contact information, and letterheads match.)

Your LinkedIn profile

As already discussed, LinkedIn is crucial, so make sure your profile is up-to-date and ready for your face-to-face contacts to peruse. You'll also need a personalized "vanity URL" (web address) for your LinkedIn profile—it looks great on your business card and resume. (See the section on LinkedIn for instructions on how to create your personalized LinkedIn URL.)

Your business card

Yes, you heard me, nursing professionals—you, yes you, need a business card. Whether you're employed or not, your business card is a piece of career-building real estate whose importance cannot be overstated.

If you happen to have a business card from your place of employment, that's fine, but I still recommend having a personal business card since the card from your workplace won't include your LinkedIn profile URL, personal email address, and other vital information. And if you're shopping for another job, you probably don't want your new contacts calling or emailing you at work, anyway.

Your business card needs to contain your name, credentials, email address, phone number, and the personalized URL of your LinkedIn profile.

You can have your card printed at a local shop, which I highly recommended in terms of supporting the local economy. You can also use one of those ubiquitous cheap printing websites, which shall remain nameless. One disadvantage of those online printing websites is that so many people use the same designs, and if your card looks exactly like fifty others, isn't it more likely to get lost in the crowd? If you want to invest just a little more, create something unique with the help of a local designer or print shop, and it will be well worth the investment.

INSPIRED ACTION

If you have a resume, set a deadline for reviewing and updating it, or hiring a professional to do so.

Mark the dates on your calendar when most of us turn the clocks ahead or back for Daylight Saving Time and Standard Time. Write "resume" on those dates to remind you of your task. (For those of you in Arizona, do this anyway, even though your state doesn't recognize Daylight Saving Time.)

If you have a basic cover letter, set a deadline for reviewing and updating it, or hiring a professional to do so.

If you don't have your own business card, set a deadline for when it will be created, printed, and delivered to your door.

Professional contact information

Having professional contact information is often overlooked, and it drives me nuts. We're professionals, aren't we? And you notice that I said "professional contact information," not "amateur contact information," right? I said that for a reason.

An email address stands out on your business card or resume, and potential colleagues or employers may contact you there. Make sure your email is professional, like *Jane-*

SmithRN@gmail.com, not *ilovekittycats@yahoo.com*, or *nurse-fromhell@hotmail.com*. Please don't ignore this, since it is part and parcel of your personal branding. While a pithy email moniker may be fun, it's not meant for professional purposes.

Your email address needs to look professional, and I recommend using Gmail for this purpose, especially since it's easy to have it automatically forwarded to another personal email address. If you have a common name and Gmail says it's taken, try adding your middle initial, placing your last name before your first name, or placing a dot between the names, like John.L.Jones@gmail.com. You can also try Jones-JohnRNBSN@gmail.com, or any combination therein. Also, make sure you have an email signature with your professional contact information and credentials at the bottom of all outgoing emails. This is easy to create in any email platform.

If you like to have ring-back tones, music, or silly sayings on your outgoing voicemail message, that's fine, but then please don't use your personal phone for professional reasons. If you open a Gmail account like I recommend, you'll also have access to Google Voice, and this allows you to have your own free Google Voice phone number. You can create a professional outgoing message on that number's voicemail, and you can easily program Google Voice to send you transcriptions of your incoming voicemail. You can also receive texts and emails with an alert that you have a new message. Incoming Google Voice calls can be directly forwarded to your personal phone, and voice messages can then be archived like emails for future reference.

If you decide to use your personal phone and voicemail for professional networking purposes, you need to have an outgoing message that says something like this:

"Hi. You've reached the voicemail of John Jones. I appreciate your call, but I'm not available at the moment. Please leave a message, and I'll return your call within 24 hours."

INSPIRED ACTION

Do you have an email address that looks professional? If not, set a deadline for creating one (and make sure your email signature contains all your contact information, credentials, etc.).

Does every email you send have an email signature containing your name, credentials, and contact information, including your LinkedIn URL? Set a date to have this completed and ready to go.

Is your outgoing voicemail message professional? Does it state your name clearly so that the caller knows who they've reached? If not, set a deadline for making your phone presence more professional.

Other tools:

Kevin Ross, my friend, business partner, and intrepid co-host at RNFM Radio, loves to talk tech, and he's fond of certain apps. I also have my favorite apps, and we frequently recommend the ones we currently rely on to keep our lives afloat and organized.

I recommend using Evernote (Evernote.com) for archiving links related to nursing, your career, facilities you want to research or visit, articles, blog posts, podcasts, videos, and other media. Evernote is great for organizing both your personal life and your career.

If you create a Gmail account, I also recommend using Google Drive, where you can have your own personal cloud-based drive that allows you to store documents, spreadsheets, and other important information for your career development and management.

Finally, I recommend Azendoo (Azendoo.com), a project management app that works in tandem with Google Drive and Evernote. On Azendoo, you can keep track of career-related tasks, your professional and personal to-do lists, and even your networking process and contacts. Azendoo is like a very robust to-do list, with links to your Evernote and Google Drive apps, programmable due dates, and folders that you can share with others.

Evernote, Azendoo, and Google Drive can all be utilized on most mobile devices, so you can have your vital information with you wherever you go.

There are plenty of other apps and tools out there as well; I just happen to like this particular trio of awesome applications. Ask around, do some research, and find what works best for you and your lifestyle. Oh, and by the way, they all have free versions that are perfectly user-friendly and robust without your ever spending a dime.

INSPIRED ACTION

Check out Evernote, Azendoo, and Google Drive, and evaluate whether they may work for you. If not, ask your tech-friendly colleagues for their recommendations. You can also explore the innumerable options available online.

Seminars, Meetings, and Conferences

Just about every nurse needs to earn CEUs during his or her career. While many of those credits can be earned through a multitude of online platforms, live conferences and seminars are opportunities not to be disregarded by the forward-thinking nurse who is keen to build a robust professional network.

In this era of quick fixes, it's easy to amass a bunch of CEU credits by logging onto an educational website and downloading your certificates, and that's fine. However, for the chance to rub shoulders and pick the brains of other like-minded nurses, attending live events is a fantastic way to give yourself—and your networking strategy—a significant boost.

These events can be multi-day conferences focusing on one nursing specialty, the meeting of a particular nursing association or group, or a local state nursing association chapter meeting. No matter what they are, these events can all be approached with the same level of professional curiosity and networking know-how.

Local Nurse Meetings:

If your state nursing association has regional or local chapters that hold meetings in your immediate area, this is a great place to start networking with other nurses who live relatively nearby.

National nursing associations—like the American Holistic Nurses Association (AHNA) or the National Association of Hispanic Nurses (NAHN)—may also have chapters that you can visit or join. Groups that have a special focus or mission can be the perfect place to meet nursing professionals who may share your values, goals, and professional outlook.

You may also hear about CEU courses and other educational opportunities being held at hotels or meeting spaces in your local area. If you attend a conference or seminar on a special area of clinical focus or nursing practice (like dementia care or integrative medicine), you may very well find yourself meeting other nurses who share your interests.

There's nothing like meeting nurses and healthcare professionals who live nearby, and your shared bond of living in

close proximity will afford very different opportunities for
connection than meeting nurses at conferences in far-flung
places around the country or the world.

Making the Most of Larger Nursing Conferences

When I go to nursing seminars and conferences, I pretend
that I'm a sponge, soaking up everything I possibly can,
including new friendships and professional connections.

During talks and presentations, I sit toward the front of
the room and take notes on my laptop or tablet rather than
on paper that can easily get lost. I caution against taking notes
on the conference agenda or other loose papers, as these can
easily disappear. Special nuggets of information or contact
information are better saved in a place that's evergreen and
secure. Some nurses I've met have a notebook just for notes
taken during these types of events, but I still prefer a digital
platform for my personal note taking.

During breaks, I obviously take care of myself with
snacks, hydration, or a few minutes outside. However, I also
use these opportunities to mingle, "work the room," and
meet other nurses and professionals who seem interesting
and open to conversation. I always have business cards in
my pocket, and some of these meetings can result in a chat
over coffee, breaking bread together, and even long-lasting
personal or professional relationships and friendships.

What to Bring to a Nursing Conference

When attending a conference or seminar, I recommend
always having your business cards with you. If you have a

business card from your place of employment, that'll do, but please bring your personal card as well.

If you happen to be in the job market, it's never a bad idea to have a few pristine, laser-printed copies of your resume on hand. And if you want to go one step further, you can have each copy in a handsome folder along with your business card. Again, you never know who you might connect with at a conference.

Network Like Crazy (or Not)

Nursing conferences and seminars are like having your very own brain trust in the room with you. Whether it's a general conference or one geared toward a specific nursing specialty, the minds in that room are like a collective treasure trove of information, connections, and expertise, and your job is to connect like crazy, if you choose to do so.

Say you're at the annual conference of *The Infusion Nurses Society* (where I happened to speak when it was held in Phoenix, Arizona, in 2014). If you're a nurse who wants to break into that specialty, this is your chance to meet nurses from all over the world who have connections, expertise, and experience that can be of benefit to you in myriad ways. If you're already an infusion nurse, and you're attending to freshen up your knowledge and connect more deeply with your area of nursing specialization, the brain trust at the conference is still yours for the asking.

When you're at a nursing conference or seminar, there are other nurses in attendance who have something to share. If you're a stranger to the group, you're faced with a slight chal-

62 Savvy Networking for Nurses

lenge in terms of working the room. If you're a known entity at that conference, you can reconnect with colleagues you haven't seen for a while, but you can also meet the new attendees, or those you haven't had the chance to meet in the past.

Having said that, if you're a more introverted person, you may not feel like networking like crazy; you may be more content to sit back, observe, and be very choosy about who you connect with. That's great, and honestly, one excellent new contact you build a good rapport with could be much more beneficial for you than fifteen superficial connections that aren't given enough time to coalesce. It's about personal style and comfort level; and for you, one superb connection may be all you need.

Speakers and presenters who attend conferences frequently want to actively meet the attendees for a variety of reasons. For one, they may simply enjoy meeting other nurses, and they may also have a booth in the exhibition all where they are selling books, products, or services that may be of interest to the participants. Meeting a famous or less-than-famous speaker can be fun and exciting, and you never know what might come of these conversations.

I've seen nurses land jobs by networking with employers at their exhibition booths. Adding to the fun, the fringe benefit of exhibition halls is the great schwag you can walk away with and bring home to your friends and family. Make the most of such interactions—and have that business card handy!

When you make a nice connection with someone at a conference or meeting, be certain to exchange business cards, and suggest that you connect on LinkedIn and other social media platforms, like Twitter and Facebook. If you're both carrying smartphones, log on while you're still together and get connected right then and there, especially on LinkedIn.

If any of these connections feel even more pregnant with potential, suggest meeting for coffee, a meal, or a walk during the conference. Exchange cell phone numbers right away, and agree to text one another in order to efficiently make arrangements.

If you're not sure what to say when meeting someone and wanting to connect, here are a few ideas you can use to craft your own introductory remarks:

> *"I'm fascinated by what you do. Would you mind grabbing a cup of coffee so I can learn more about your nursing career?"*

> *"I love meeting other nurses and learning about what they do; that's one reason I come to these conferences. Would you like to have lunch? I have a feeling we have a lot in common!"*

> *"I'm intrigued by what you've said about your career. Can we sit down over coffee and chat? I'm really interested to learn more!"*

Did you notice that in the three examples above the speaker never said anything about what he or she wanted, other than learning about the other person? Showing authentic interest is key, and your curiosity can be your guide in being open to meeting interesting new connections.

Choosing Where and What to Attend

Whether you attend a three-day conference in an enormous urban hotel, a local nursing association chapter meeting, a five-day nurses' cruise, or a one-day seminar in your hometown, these in-person nursing events are your chance to make professional and personal connections that may prove to be lifelong.

The people you meet at conferences and seminars are your colleagues, potential friends and employers, and possibly people who can be your mentors or guides along your career path. Scores of nurses attend conferences and meetings for reasons of learning and networking, and you can rest assured that the majority are happy to meet and chat with other nurses in attendance.

Earning CEUs is great, but the gold of nursing conferences, meetings, and seminars is the relationships that are forged and the learning that can take place. Make use of these opportunities for the benefit of your career and your ever-expanding professional network.

With our current ability to access virtually
unlimited information from almost anywhere,
at almost any time, the need to understand
professional online networking skills could
not be more crucial or salient.

CHAPTER 5

Online Networking Savvy

THE ONLINE WORLD has changed enormously from its humble but exciting beginnings in the 1990s. In the days of dial-up Internet and super-slow desktop computers, the notion of social media was still just barely a twinkle in the eye of some visionary denizen of the techie world Little did we know how it would alter our lives so indelibly.

The Internet is the center of the known universe for many of us, and we now carry powerful miniature computers in our pockets—computers cleverly disguised as smart phones. With our current ability to access virtually unlimited information from almost anywhere at almost any time, the need to understand professional online networking skills could not be more salient.

In terms of online networking, LinkedIn is arguably the most important tool to master, and other social media platforms then follow in varying degrees of relevance, including

Twitter, Facebook, Instagram, and others. For astute nurses, LinkedIn, Twitter, and Facebook appear to be the online destinations where the majority of nurses spend their time connecting, although Instagram (which is owned by Facebook) is gaining traction.

LinkedIn was purchased by Microsoft in 2016 for an enormous amount of money. With alterations to the user interface slowly rolling out over time, there are grumblings that the changes are not all for the better. Indeed, some of my favorite functions have either been removed entirely or are now only available with a Premium account. You can expect that the platform may continue to change, and some of the instructions and screenshots in this chapter may eventually be less useful. After all, when you write about technology, you have to be prepared for that technology to evolve.

Speaking of Premium LinkedIn accounts, I still don't have one, and I advise you to weigh the cost carefully before purchasing. Premium is great for recruiters, but you can accomplish a great deal with a free account. Start small, keep it simple, and leverage your free LinkedIn presence as much as you can before investing in Premium.

We'll begin with LinkedIn, and then delve into other online platforms that may suit your needs, temperament, skills, and interest.

 LinkedIn and You

The Reality

- LinkedIn is currently the most powerful professional online networking tool available. This is unlikely to change in the foreseeable future, especially since Microsoft bought LinkedIn in 2016.
- Worldwide users number in the hundreds of millions, and this is steadily increasing.
- For building an authentic online network, there's currently nothing like it on the Internet.
- LinkedIn is actually a powerful search engine disguised as a social media platform. It serves several purposes, and the search engine is the fuel behind the LinkedIn rocket.
- Many potential employers immediately Google those who apply for positions, and examining applicants' LinkedIn profiles is a common practice.
- A small but growing number of organizations require a LinkedIn profile as part of their application process. Some highly tech-savvy companies require that applicants submit their LinkedIn profile in lieu of a resume.

What's the problem?

- Many users simply don't know how to effectively use the LinkedIn platform.
- Users ignore their profiles, leading to woefully out-of-date information.

- People "collect" connections and contacts but do nothing with them.
- Users do too much self-promotion and not enough promoting of others (this is a rampant practice on most social media platforms).
- Not following up is one of the cardinal sins of networking (this is also rampant).
- There's no excuse, or logical reason, for networking in a way that doesn't foster real relationships.
- Many people erroneously see LinkedIn as simply an online resume.
- Valuable online "real estate" is wasted by so many users who just don't know any better.

Solutions for Your LinkedIn Strategy

- Maximize your profile.
- Learn how to use keywords to enhance your visibility.
- Search for kindred spirits and colleagues, and invite them to connect through personalized invitations.
- Enhance connections with those users you feel most aligned with by offering to connect via phone, Skype, or FaceTime, or even in person.
- Build relationships by sharing and connecting with others.
- Endorse, recommend, and support others.
- Request (and give) recommendations.
- Use LinkedIn Pulse (the native LinkedIn blogging platform) to write articles that showcase your expertise.

- Join groups and take part in discussions.
- Start your own LinkedIn group.
- Follow companies and brands you admire.

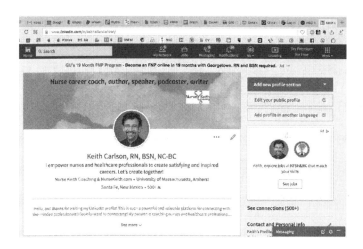

It all begins with your profile

Your LinkedIn profile is your professional window on the world. It showcases who you are, what you do, what you've done, and who you're connected with. Your profile can be minimal, elaborate, or somewhere in between. I recommend making your profile as robust, informative, and inviting as possible, while remaining consummately professional.

Once you've created a profile (or you're ready to enhance the profile you started in 2009 and have been quietly ignoring ever since), I find it best to work from the top down.

Your LinkedIn profile consists of various discrete sections that serve specific purposes, and they each deserve your loving attention, not to mention consistent feeding and watering.

These are the basic building blocks of the top section of
your profile:

- Headshot
- Name and title
- Headline
- Contact information
- Professional summary

The headshot is simple when you have a smartphone. If
you don't want to spend money on a professional photogra-
pher, do a photo shoot with a friend who has a good eye and
a steady hand. A simple head-and-shoulders photo of you
smiling and looking directly at the camera is perfect.

LinkedIn doesn't have a separate dialog box to put your
credentials, so when you're entering your name in your
profile, just type your credentials after your last name. You
worked hard for those letters, so flaunt them!

Your headline is the little blurb under your photo and
name. You can, of course, write "Registered Nurse," but
feel free to be more creative. If you have special experience
or qualifications, use this space to tell people who you are
and what makes you unique. For example, you could write,
"Experienced RN certified in wound care and ostomies,"
"Registered Nurse with expertise in diabetes education and
cardiac care," or "Travel nurse who'd just rather live in Bali
and write the great American novel." You want to capture
their attention.

A good way to learn about LinkedIn profiles is to look at
the profiles of other people and assess what you like and don't

like (believe me, there's plenty of both). Peruse 30 or 40 and you'll know which ones are interesting and which ones are like fallow ground waiting for water (or at least a long overdue visit from the gardener). There are also countless websites, ebooks, video tutorials, webinars, and other opportunities to take your LinkedIn use into the digital stratosphere.

You can also engage a LinkedIn expert in one-on-one LinkedIn coaching. Since I just happen to have a unique perspective as the only LinkedIn expert who is also a nurse entrepreneur, you're welcome to contact me for a chat about how we could work and play together in the world of LinkedIn.

Your social media platforms are only as good as the information you populate them with, so get with the program and plant your seeds with care. And when you create a profile, I'll be checking to make sure you don't neglect it! (Just kidding. sort of.)

Creating Your LinkedIn Profile URL

Since revamping the LinkedIn user interface, Microsoft has indeed made it easier to create your personalized URL. With your profile open, you'll see a blue box in the right-hand column labeled "Add new profile section." Just underneath that, click "Edit your public profile." On the right, you'll see "Edit public profile URL." This is your ticket to personalization.

All LinkedIn URLs begin with "LinkedIn.com/in/." After that second slash, you can add whatever you'd like your URL to be. If your name is already taken, try putting your last name first and your first name last. If that doesn't work,

add your middle initial, or perhaps "RN" or other credentials.
For example:

- LinkedIn.com/in/marysmithbsn
- LinkedIn.com/in/smithmaryrn
- LinkedIn.com/in/maryjanesmithrn

Once created, this is the web address you can put on your
resume, cover letters, letterhead, and business card to demon-
strate that you're a savvy 21st-century nursing professional.
Note: When writing your LinkedIn URL on a business card,
letterhead, resume, or other document, I recommend capi-
talizing your names and credentials because it just looks nicer
in printed form. You can also skip the "www." For example:
LinkedIn.com/in/MarySmithBSN.

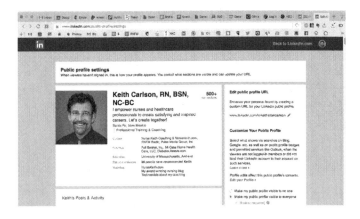

Connecting

So, you may ask, how could you possibly develop symbiotic
and authentic relationships with every connection on LinkedIn?
The simple answer is that you can't. You wouldn't have time

for anything else. Having said that, if it's indeed your intention to find those people with whom you have some modicum of connection and like-minded professional goals and aspirations, you're off to a great start.

To create authentic connections with some of your LinkedIn contacts, one rule I always follow is to never send an impersonal, generic invitation. If I want to invite someone to be in my circle, I first read through their profile and learn something about them.

The new LinkedIn interface makes connecting easier than it used to be. On each user's profile you'll see a blue button labeled "Connect." When you click it, you'll be given the option to "Send now" or "Add a note." Always choose "Add a note" and tell them why you're reaching out. (You'll also be given the choice to send an "InMail," but this is only for Premium users.) If you don't see the "Connect" button, you'll find three little horizontal dots that, when clicked, reveal a dropdown menu with an option to connect.

INSPIRED ACTION

Connect with me on LinkedIn by sending me a personalized invitation. I generally don't respond to generic invitations unless they happen to be from someone I know. As of this writing I have more than 400 invitations I haven't responded to, so if connecting with me is important to you, make it personal. My LinkedIn URL is https://linkedin.com/in/keithallancarlson.)

Once your invitation is accepted (which is relatively likely), you can begin to court that individual via the LinkedIn email system. Once that connection is established, I usually request that we move our communications to our personal email addresses and out of LinkedIn, mostly because regular email is easier to track and archive.

With some LinkedIn contacts, my attempts at communication aren't terribly fruitful, but there are many people I've spoken with on the phone or Skype, or even met in person when one of us is visiting the area where the other lives, or we're attending the same conference or event. You can't be best friends with everyone, but making some deeper connections can be fun, enlightening, and potentially advantageous to your career.

Speaking of meeting your contacts in person, LinkedIn provides handy tools for searching for new contacts based on various indices (location, employer, role, etc.). Some LinkedIn users will get in touch with contacts in a city they're about to visit and set up meetings. Speaking from personal experience, this can be quite enjoyable.

To search on LinkedIn, click on the search bar in the upper left corner, and then click on the magnifying glass. In the right-hand column, you'll see a filter function that allows you to search by location, keywords, companies, industries, and other variables. If you want to connect with Chief Nursing Officers in the greater Minneapolis area, you can actually do that. And if you want to find every LinkedIn user connected with Johns Hopkins you can do that too. Enjoy playing with this feature and you'll find yourself creating new relationships and connections like a pro.

Joining groups on LinkedIn is yet another method for meeting and getting to know like-minded colleagues and peers. When you join a LinkedIn group, you immediately have ready access to every other member, and this gives you a perfect ground to build a relationship with another member of the group and begin discussing what you have in common.

There are many insider tricks in the advanced use of LinkedIn. For now, if you focus on creating a great profile, reaching out to other users you feel some affinity with, and building authentic, symbiotic relationships over time, you've taken more advantage of LinkedIn than most users ever will.

LinkedIn is the go-to online platform for professional networking, so use it to its fullest functionality and enjoy the fruits of your networking labors.

 ## The Twitterverse

For those of you who feel that Twitter is a superficial online universe where people write pithy messages about celebrity plastic surgery disasters in 140 characters or less, I'd love an opportunity to convince you otherwise.

Twitter is a healthy and active social media network, and if you learn how to use the platform intelligently, useful relationships can indeed be born from those 140-character interactions. Believe me, it's true.

Twitter has fueled revolutions, assisted in disaster relief, and connected activists, organizers, job-seekers, professionals, and a plethora of individuals and groups seeking allies and timely information. It happens all the time.

My Story

One day in late 2011, I was hanging out on Twitter, chatting with a number of nurses and nurse entrepreneurs who were lighting up various hashtags related to our profession. (Hashtags are terms preceded by a "#" symbol, which makes them searchable through the aggregation of tweets using that hashtag. For example, "#nurse" or "#nursing" are used by nurses thousands of times per day, and many of us follow those hashtags for breaking news and information.)

Anyway, I met a nurse entrepreneur named Anna Morrison who seemed very interesting. We apparently had a great deal in common, so we connected on Facebook and LinkedIn, exchanged email addresses, and were chatting on the phone in short order. Lo and behold, we quickly discovered that we both wanted to start a podcast about nursing, so Anna brought her Twitter friend Kevin Ross, the well-known nurse entrepreneur, into the conversation. He and I were already aware of one another's presence, but had not interacted directly.

This nascent three-way alliance was so strong that after one marathon Skype session, we launched our podcast, RNFM Radio. Anna subsequently left the show to go back to school, but Kevin and I have been going strong ever since, and we've even formed a company together and taken part in a variety of mutual ventures. All of this was born from Anna and me noticing one another's Twitter-based positivity and enthusiasm regarding the nursing profession. Superficial connection? Hardly! Remunerative and fun? You bet!

A lot can be said for the brevity of tweets, and when you take into consideration the entirety of an individual's Twitter presence, you can actually surmise a great deal about them over time. For this reason, I count many nurses and nurse entrepreneurs in the Twitterverse as my friends, and I've actually met some of them in person at conferences and seminars over the years, just as I have with my LinkedIn community.

Speaking of hashtags, a phenomenon known as a "tweetchat" can fire up on Twitter almost every day, and many tweetchats are directly related to nursing, medicine, and health care. During a tweetchat, the "conversation" takes place at a predetermined time, with Twitter users logging on and following the tweetchat's hashtag in real time. For example, if the tweetchat's chosen hashtag is "#ivnursing," those interested in the conversation will enter that hashtag in the Twitter search bar, and then refresh their search every few minutes. Meanwhile, every tweet meant to be part of that conversation has the "#ivnursing" hashtag within the message. An ongoing conversation will occur, and you'd

be amazed how nurses from around the world will simul-
taneously and actively take part in that conversation. It's a
fascinating 21st-century form of communication, and the
discussions can be lively and informative.

INSPIRED ACTION

Create a Twitter account and follow me, @nursekeith.
Then type "#nurse" and "#nursing" in the search
bar and see what nurses are talking about.

If you're hanging out on Twitter and begin to interact
with another nurse or professional, you can, of course, invite
that person to connect with you via email, and you can also
find them on LinkedIn and perhaps become friends on Facebook. If the connection is strong, you might chat on the
phone, have a Skype session, or maybe even meet in person
when you're in the same city or attending the same event.

Think of Twitter as an enormous cocktail party that you
can attend in your pajamas. On Twitter, you can stand by
the wall as a passive observer, or you can assertively work
the room, meeting as many people as you care to. Luckily,
no one can see what you're wearing, and you don't have to
comb your hair, shave, or put on makeup. And when you're
ready to leave the party, you don't even have to let the hostess
know that you need to get home before the kids set fire to
the house, tie up the babysitter, and sell her jewelry on eBay.
You just exit, stage left.

Thousands of nurses use Twitter for both personal and professional reasons, and like any other networking platform, you pretty much get out of it what you put in. So, invest your time and energy on Twitter, and you may very well come out feeling like a networking alchemist, even though you're wearing Sponge Bob pajamas and pink bunny rabbit slippers.

 Facebook

Many of us have a love-hate (or like-unlike) relationship with Facebook, and I completely understand the sentiment. Due to Facebook's periodic privacy-related debacles, many users have indeed switched to other social media platforms, and some of us simply hang in there because it's useful, user-friendly, and ultimately a big help to us in various aspects of our lives.

With vehement foes, gushing fans, and ambivalent prisoners, Facebook is frequently in the news, and in case you haven't noticed, many brands and corporate entities of various sizes also have a Facebook presence. For nurse entrepreneurs, having your brand represented on Facebook is pretty much required, and I personally recommend it.

We all make choices when it comes to social media, but if you're a nurse entrepreneur with a desire to connect with other nurses, you simply have to realize that an appreciable variety of nurses spend time on Facebook. In Facebook's nursing world, there are open groups, secret groups, and all manner of ways nurses share information. Some nurses have personal Facebook pages that are strictly personal, and some focus more on connections with other nurses and not so much on friends and family.

If you want to socialize with other nurses on social media, Facebook is in the batter's box, following Twitter and LinkedIn. Again, those relationships can be migrated to the phone, Skype, email, and face-to-face meetings when possible. We nurses need to bear in mind that Facebook is the main social media space for millions of users. We don't know if Facebook will ever be supplanted as the go-to social media platform on the Internet, but we can safely assume that its influence as a social media juggernaut will be felt for years to come. Use Facebook to your advantage.

Other Platforms

Aside from the trifecta of LinkedIn, Twitter, and Facebook, some nurses engage on other social media platforms, such as Instagram, Reddit, Pinterest, WhatsApp, Tumblr, YouTube, and others. Nurses, feel free to peruse them during your oodles of free time.

Specialized social media sites have been consistently created for nurses since the dawn of the Internet, and these platforms have come and gone for years. Due to the variable longevity and relevance of these sites, I will refrain from mentioning any by name since they are apt to appear and disappear with dizzying speed.

Having said that, watch for the emergence of a new nursing site or platform that appears to offer a solid opportunity for networking with other nurses, and jump aboard if it feels right. However, understand the caveat that many of these sites don't last, and the data you enter may be lost forever when they're flushed down the digital toilet. User, beware.

Networking is indeed all about relationships,

and if those relationships are symbiotic and fun,

all the better for everyone.

CHAPTER 6

Final Thoughts

I F YOU TAKE AWAY nothing from this book other than the following point, I've still done my job: *it's all about relationships*. Networking is indeed all about relationships, and if those relationships are symbiotic and fun, all the better for everyone.

If you're not used to networking, this brave new world may seem overwhelming, to say the least. It's so easy to just stay in your little nursing unit, ignore the rest of the world, and allow time to pass you by. I get it, and that's actually what many people do every day.

My hope is that this book has persuaded you that networking—both online and in person—is a process most professionals should be regularly engaged in. I will readily admit that there are always exceptions to every rule, and you're absolutely free to make your own determination of what works for you. However, for most professionals interested in a long, productive, and satisfying career, networking can be fun, engaging, enjoyable, and enormously productive.

In the course of your career (or perhaps after reading this very book), some of you will feel intrinsically drawn to online networking, while the act of face-to-face networking will have all the attractiveness of being on the receiving end of a colonoscopy. In fact, some of you would probably prefer the colonoscopy. (But have you ever had cheap white wine and chips and salsa in a colonoscopy suite? Just sayin'.)

But seriously, for those died-in-the-wool introverts out there, face-to-face networking may simply be forever *verboten*, so in that case, lean hard into online networking and build your collection of wonderful professional connections from that vantage point.

For those readers who are loathe to immerse themselves in the sea of LinkedIn, Twitter, Facebook, or other popular social media platforms, I encourage you to choose just one, and dip your toe into the networking waters.

Networking is simply in your best interests as a professional, and I hope I've inspired you to give it a go. Most importantly, have fun and make friends, and come to the world of networking with the goal of embodying authenticity and generating symbiotic connections. If that's your *modus operandi*, you can't go wrong.

I hope to meet you out there in the big old digital and three-dimensional worlds, and I wish you all the best as you create, nurture, and cultivate a professional network that will enhance your life in ways that you can only begin to imagine.

Have fun, and keep in touch!

About the Author

Keith Carlson, RN, BSN, NC-BC is a holistic career coach for nurses, award-winning nurse blogger, writer, consultant, podcaster, speaker, author, and popular career columnist. He is a Board Certified Nurse Coach (NC-BC) under the auspices of the American Holistic Nurses Credentialing Corporation.

With two decades of nursing experience, Keith deeply understands the issues faced by 21st-century nurses. He provides expert career coaching that guides nurses, nurse entrepreneurs, and healthcare professionals on the path to a fulfilling career.

Keith has written for Nurse.com, Nurse.org, Working Nurse Magazine, Multibriefs News Service, American Sentinel University, StaffGarden, and many other online platforms. He has also contributed chapters to a number of books about nursing and healthcare.

With a powerful message of savvy career management and professional satisfaction that reaches tens of thousands of nurses worldwide, Keith can be found on his blog, Digital Doorway, as well as Facebook, Twitter, LinkedIn, Instagram, and at NurseKeith.com. His popular podcasts, The Nurse Keith Show and RNFM Radio, reach nurses on six continents.

Based in beautiful Santa Fe, New Mexico with his lovely wife and stunningly adorable and intelligent cat, Keith enjoys time with elders, children, animals, and the occasional adult.

Also by Keith "Nurse Keith" Carlson

Aspire to be Inspired: Creating a Nursing Career That Matters" (2017)

Keith is a contributing author in the following books:

Final Moments: Nurses' Stories about Death and Dying, edited by Deborah Witt Sherman, PhD, APRN. (Kaplan, 2009).

Reflections on Doctors: Nurses' Stories about Physicians and Surgeons, edited by Terry Ratner, RN, MFA. (Kaplan, 2008).

Nurses on the Run: Why They Come, Why They Stay, edited by Karen Buley, RN, BSN. (Dog Ear Publishing, 2009).

Successful Nurse Communication: Safe Care, Healthy Workplaces, and Rewarding Careers, by Beth Boynton. (F.A. Davis, 2016).

How to Find Keith

NurseKeith.com
Facebook.com/NurseKeithCoaching
Twitter.com/NurseKeith
LinkedIn.com/in/keithallancarlson
RNFMRadio.com

THE NURSE KEITH SHOW:
http://nursekeithshow.libsyn.com

Savvy Networking For Nurses was designed by Ann Lowe (www.graphicdesignforbooks.com), and edited by Jeffrey Braucher (www.santafeworddoctor.com).

Made in the USA
Columbia, SC
20 March 2018